4.1

NoLC4 4114

PEACHTREE CITY LIBRARY
201 Willowbend Road
Peachtree City, GA 30269-1623
Phone: 770-631-2520
Fax: 770-631-2522

IF YOU GIVE AN AUTHOR A PENCIL

by

Laura Numeroff

photographs by

Sherry Shahan

Richard C. Owen Publishers, Inc.
Katonah, New York

Meet The Author

Richard C. Owen Publishers, Inc.
PO Box 585
Katonah, New York 10536

Library of Congress Cataloging-in-Publication Data

Numeroff, Laura Joffe.
    If you give an author a pencil / by Laura Numeroff ; photographs by Sherry Shahan.
        p. cm. — (Meet the author)
    Summary: Author Laura Numeroff, whose first book, "Amy for Short," grew out of a college assignment, recounts her life and describes how her daily activities and creative process are interwoven.
    ISBN 1-57274-595-9
    1. Numeroff, Laura Joffe—Juvenile literature. 2. Authors, American—20th century—Biography—Juvenile literature. 3. Children's stories—Authorship—Juvenile literature. [1. Numeroff, Laura Joffe. 2. Authors, American.] I. Shahan, Sherry, ill. II. Title. III. Series. IV. Meet the author (Katonah, N.Y.)

PS3564.U45 Z468 2002
[E]—dc21
                                                        2002074266

Editorial, Art, and Production Director *Janice Boland*
Production Assistants *Donna Parsons, Elaine Kemp*
Administrative Assistance *Janet Lipareli*

Color separations by Leo P. Callahan, Inc., Binghamton, NY

Printed in the United States of America

9   8   7   6   5   4   3

For fellow readers everywhere

Dear Readers,

When I was a child, I wrote to an author
and he sent me a response. I was thrilled!

Now I'm the one getting letters from children
asking about my life.
What an honor!

Dear MS Numeroff,

Hi my mame is Jenny. I love your book. MY favorite book is If You Give a Mouse a Cookie, thats the book You wrote.

How long did it take you to write the book? How do You feel about the book? I Loved the book So So much that I am telling everbody even You that I like this great interesting cook.

How did you draw the book? I wish I could meet you face to face. Do You really love the book If You Give a mouse a cookie? MY favorite Part was when the mouse was acting So So thirsty.

Your friend
Jennifer
P.S. Please write back soon.

I was born on July 14th,
French Independence Day.
I'm not French but
sometimes I wish I were.
Ooh la la!

I'm the youngest of three girls. My sisters are Alice and
Emily. When I was born they helped my mother
pick my name, which I love.

I enjoyed growing up in Brooklyn, New York, in the fifties. This is the house where I spent my childhood. My family and I lived upstairs and my grandmother lived downstairs. She was our built-in baby-sitter.

Our house was filled with books, music, and art.
My mother Florence taught home economics
in junior high school. She and my father loved
to go square dancing and folk dancing.
They even gave dance lessons in our basement.
I remember evenings filled with music and lively dancing.

My father William was a very skilled artist.
He also loved to read. Soon, reading and drawing
were two of my favorite things to do.

I took all kinds of
lessons: piano, tap
dancing, ballet, and
guitar. But the ones I
liked most were the
drawing lessons.

I spent a lot of time at museums, zoos,
and the library with my family.
I will never forget my first library card.
What a treat to have such a choice of books.
I took out as many as they allowed and went back
for more every week.

My four all-time favorite books were
Cat in the Hat, Eloise, Stuart Little,
and *Misty of Chincoteague.*
I loved book series and biographies.

When I turned nine, I started writing stories
and drawing pictures to go with them.
That's when I first knew I wanted to be a writer.

But when I was fifteen, I decided to follow
a different path. I wanted to be just like
my big sister, Emily, who was a fashion designer.
I even went to the same college, Pratt Institute,
in Brooklyn, New York.

After my first year studying fashion,
I realized it wasn't for me.
Besides, I couldn't sew at all.

I tried animation but I knew it wasn't
something that I wanted to spend my life doing.

Then I studied photography.
Even though I loved it, I just didn't want
to be a full-time photographer.

I ended up taking a class at Pratt called
Writing and Illustrating Children's Books.
It was fun. My teacher was Barbara Bottner,
a children's book author and illustrator.
I wanted to be just like her.

Barbara gave us a homework assignment:
to write and illustrate our own book.
Mine was about a girl who was the tallest
in her third grade class.
(No, I wasn't the tallest in my third grade class.)
I called my book *Amy for Short.*

Barbara said I did a good job. I got so excited,
I tried to sell it. And I did.

After four rejections, a big publisher
bought my homework.
Before I had even graduated,
I had a contract for my first book.
I immediately called my family from a phone booth
to tell them the good news.

Two years later, I took a two-week trip
to San Francisco and ended up staying
for seven years. San Francisco is
one of my favorite cities.

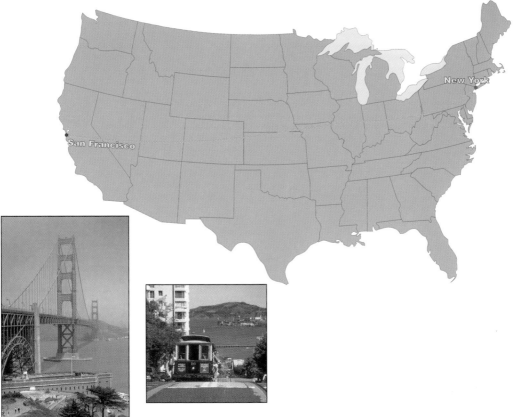

To support myself at that time
I had a lot of part-time jobs.
I was the worst receptionist, secretary,
and waitress. In between, though, I managed
to write and illustrate eight books.

VIOLET, POPPY AND BABS
by
Laura Numeroff

Violet, Poppy and Babs were sisters.

Violet was a cook at Hank's House of Pies, Poppy a math teacher and Babs
worked in a book store.

They lived in Florida in a little yellow house with a very large porch and a
roof that leaked when it rained.

Violet was the eldest. She couldn't see very well, but she loved to bake.

She had lots and lots of recipes written on index cards and tiny scraps of
paper that she stuffed into a wicker picnic basket that her Aunt Agnes gave
her.

Violet had recipes for all kinds of goodies... coconut [butterscotch] cookies with raisins
and nuts, butterscotch brownies with peanut butter frosting , lemon bars with
walnut pieces and her favorite, angel food cake with dark chocolate frosting
and sprinkles.

"Boy, do I love to bake" she would say, mixing and stirring in the sunny
kitchen.

The only problem was she couldn't read the dial on the oven, so the house was
always filled with smoke.

Poppy and Babs ate Violet's cookies and cake anyway.

"Yummy" Poppy would say, wrapping the burnt parts in her napkin when Violet
wasn't looking.

"Scrumptious" said Babs, pecking gently past the burnt edges.

It made Violet happy to see [know] her sisters enjoy [enjoyed] her baking.

Poppy was the middle sister. She loved to knit.

She knit vests with eleven pockets, twenty two foot scarves and striped
turtle neck sweaters with fringe .

"Boy, do I love to knit" she would say, sitting on the sofa, surrounded by
shopping bags full of yarn in all different colors.

She gave everything she made to Violet and Babs, except at Christmas when she
knit gifts for the neighbors.

It made Poppy happy to see [knew] her sisters enjoy [enjoyed] her knitting.

Then, on a long, boring car trip,
I got a little silly.

"What if you went to the zoo,"
I said to my friend, "and the gorilla was eating pizza?"
He laughed.

Then I said, "What if you gave a mouse a cookie?"
In my imagination I pictured a tiny mouse
nibbling on a chocolate chip cookie
(my favorite kind of cookie).

"He'd probably want some milk
to go with it," I told my friend.

I ended up telling the whole story
from beginning to end. It's the first time
that ever happened and it hasn't happened since.

When I got home, I typed *If You Give a Mouse a Cookie*
on my little portable typewriter that had no "W."
I sent my story to Harper & Row because they had published
my favorite book about a mouse, *Stuart Little*.
I loved that story because it was set in New York
where I grew up.

Harper & Row rejected my story.
So I sent it out again and again.
It was turned down eight more times.

In 1980 I moved to Los Angeles to do some writing
for television. That summer I heard there was
a new editor at Harper & Row. She was also named Laura.
That seemed like a good omen, so I sent her
If You Give a Mouse a Cookie.
She called to say she would like to publish it.

That's why my motto is "Never give up!"
What if I'd given up after the eighth rejection?

Though I was an illustrator, I decided not to illustrate
my own book. My editor, Laura Geringer,
picked Felicia Bond to do the wonderful illustrations
for *If You Give a Mouse a Cookie*.

The book was originally a single title.
I had no idea that it would be the first in a series.

I feel honored that children
everywhere seem to like my stories.
It's an incredible feeling
to see my books in different languages.

They've been published in German, Swedish,
Danish, Japanese, Korean, Chinese, Hebrew,
Italian, Afrikaans, and Spanish.

I get ideas for books in many ways.
One day, I saw a Dalmatian dog and thought
it would look cute wearing red high-top sneakers.
My imagination took off and I started rhyming
in my head.

"Dogs don't wear sneakers
and pigs don't wear hats
and dresses look silly on Siamese cats."

As soon as I got home, I sat down
at my computer and continued
making up the verses. It was so much fun
trying to imagine animals doing silly things
and wearing funny clothes!

I had to figure out the exact number of beats
in each line of verse that I was rhyming.

My trick was to make dashes on a piece of paper
for each beat, which was equal to one syllable.

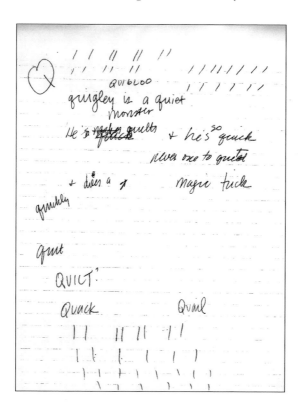

"Dogs don't wear sneakers" is five beats long,
"and pigs don't wear hats" is another five beats,
"and dresses look silly on Siamese cats"
is eleven beats. That makes one verse.

This became my formula for the rest of the book.
It's like doing a puzzle; that's why I love to rhyme.

I sent the poem to an editor but she rejected it.
(Even though you've sold a lot of books,
you can still get rejected.)

But the second editor I sent it to loved it.
He made some changes and sent it back to me.
I took some of his suggestions and did a rewrite.

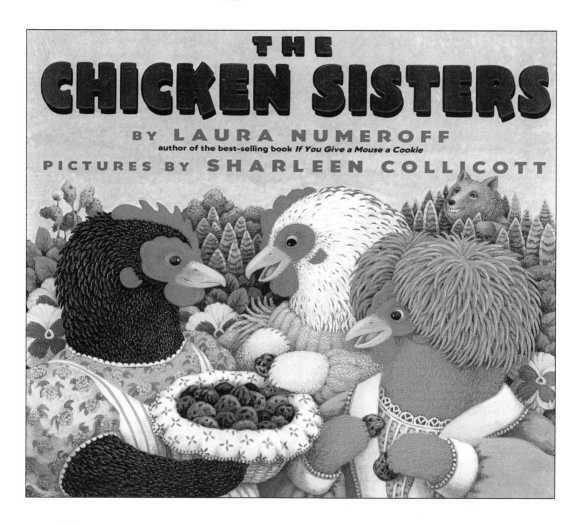

The amount of rewrites varies with each book.
If You Give a Mouse a Cookie took only two rewrites.
Chicken Sisters took fifteen!

Then it was time to choose an illustrator for
the story. My editor sent me the work of an artist,
Joe Mathieu. I loved the way he drew animals
and thought he would do a great job.
He did!

I had so much fun
writing the verses
that I ended up with
enough to make
a second book, *Chimps
Don't Wear Glasses.*

One thing I find interesting about having someone else
illustrate my stories is to see how they interpret
the words. For *Chimps Don't Wear Glasses,*
I imagined some old, fat chimps at the zoo
with reading glasses looking at newspapers.
Joe's illustration was a rock and roll band of chimpanzees
wearing wild sunglasses, which is much more fun.

Sometimes I wake up with an idea
in the middle of the night. *Monster Munchies*
came to me like that. I wonder if I was dreaming
about monsters. I hope not!

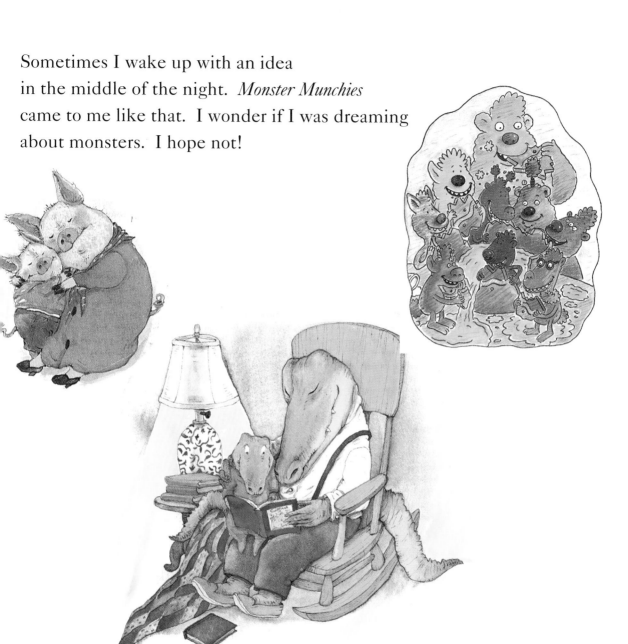

Other times I hear things that give me ideas.
I heard a mother talking about all the things
she does with her kids. That gave me the idea to write
What Mommies Do Best and *What Daddies Do Best*.

When I get an idea I immediately write it down.
It may be on the back of a napkin or on a scrap of paper.
I keep a pad in the car and in my bag beside me
all the time.

When I've completed a first draft,
I don't look at it for a few days.
When I go back to it, I read it out loud
and change the things I don't like.

She'll invite you to come along.

You'll want to get dressed up ~~and~~ so will she.

(I LIKE ALL YOUR DRESSING UP VISUALS)

Your closet for something special. *she'll look thru when shes all dressed up.*

When she's finished getting dressed, she'll want to put on a hat.

She'll look through your drawers to find one.

While she's looking, she might notice your camera.

First ~~She'll take some pictures of you.~~ *ask you*

Then she'll ask you to take some pictures of her.

She'll smile and say "Cheese".

When the pictures are ready, she'll want to send one to her friend.

She'll choose her favorite.

Then she'll ask you for an envelope and a stamp.

She'll sit at your desk to address ~~it but your desk will be too high.~~

~~You'll have to get some books for her to sit on.~~

She'll write her friends name and address.

when the envelopes ~~She'll lick the envelope and seal it.~~ *she'll want to go outside + mail them.*

~~Then she'll lick the stamp and put it on.~~

~~Licking the stamp and the envelope will make her feel sticky.~~

You'll ~~go~~ *have* *with her.*

I do that until I'm satisfied. Then I type it up and send it to an editor.

Some days I don't write at all and other days
I write for hours and hours, sometimes past midnight.

My dog, Sydney, loves to sleep under my desk.
My cats, Lily and Petunia, enjoy the warmth
of my desk lamp. I love having my pets around me.

I'm lucky that I can work at home.
Don't tell anyone, but sometimes I write in my pajamas!

When a book is published, I might go
on a book tour. I go to bookstores, visit with my readers,
and sign their books. Sometimes I'll go to ten different cities
in ten days.

It's exhausting but lots of fun.
There are only four states that I haven't been to —
Montana, Hawaii, Alaska, and Idaho.

To share my love of reading
with children and teachers,
I have visited over one hundred
elementary schools all over the country.

It makes me feel so good to know
that I'm inspiring children to write
and draw just as my father inspired me.

Happy reading!

Your friend,

Laura Numeroff

Laura Numeroff

Other Books by Laura Numeroff

Dogs Don't Wear Sneakers; If You Give a Pig a Pancake; If You Take a Mouse to School; Sometimes I Wonder If Poodles Like Noodles; If You Give a Bunny a Birthday Cake

About the Photographer

Photograph by Laura Numeroff

Sherry Shahan has taken photographs of many authors in their homes as they go about their daily activities and the business of creating their books. With her camera, Sherry recorded the things Laura Numeroff does to develop her stories from an idea into a manuscript and a published book for children to read and enjoy.

Acknowledgments

Amy for Short by Laura Numeroff appears on page 12 courtesy of Laura Numeroff. Illustration on page 15 from *If You Give a Mouse a Cookie* by Laura Numeroff, copyright ©1985 by Laura Numeroff, illustrations copyright © by Felicia Bond, used by permission of HarperCollins. Book cover on page 16 of *If You Give a Mouse a Cookie* by Laura Numeroff, copyright ©1985 by Laura Numeroff, illustrations copyright © by Felicia Bond, used by permission of HarperCollins. Book cover on page 17 of *If You Give a Moose a Cookie* by Laura Numeroff, copyright ©1991 by Laura Numeroff, illustrations copyright © by Felicia Bond, used by permission of HarperCollins. Book cover on page 21 of *Chicken Sisters* by Laura Numeroff, copyright ©1997 by Laura Numeroff, illustrations copyright © by Sharleen Collicott, used by permission of HarperCollins. Book cover on page 22 of *Chimps Don't Wear Glasses* by Laura Numeroff, copyright ©1995 by Laura Numeroff, illustrations copyright © by Joe Mathieu, used by permission of Simon and Schuster. Top illustration on page 23 from *Monster Munchies* by Laura Numeroff, copyright © 1998 by Laura Numeroff, illustrations copyright © by Nate Evans, used by permission of Random House. Middle illustration on page 23 from *What Mommies Do Best* by Laura Numeroff, copyright ©2002 by Laura Numeroff, illustrations copyright © by Lynn Munsinger, used by permission of Simon and Schuster Books for Young Readers. Bottom illustration on page 23 from *What Daddies Do Best* by Laura Numeroff, copyright ©2002 by Laura Numeroff, illustrations copyright © by Lynn Munsinger, used by permission of Simon and Schuster Books for Young Readers.

Meet the Author titles

Verna Aardema   *A Bookworm Who Hatched*
David A. Adler   *My Writing Day*
Frank Asch   *One Man Show*
Joseph Bruchac   *Seeing the Circle*
Eve Bunting   *Once Upon a Time*
Lynne Cherry   *Making a Difference in the World*
Lois Ehlert   *Under My Nose*
Denise Fleming   *Maker of Things*
Douglas Florian   *See for Your Self*
Jean Fritz   *Surprising Myself*
Paul Goble   *Hau Kola Hello Friend*
Ruth Heller   *Fine Lines*
Lee Bennett Hopkins   *The Writing Bug*
James Howe   *Playing With Words*
Johanna Hurwitz   *A Dream Come True*
Eric A. Kimmel   *Tuning Up*
Karla Kuskin   *Thoughts, Pictures, and Words*
Thomas Locker   *The Man Who Paints Nature*
Jonathan London   *Tell Me a Story*
George Ella Lyon   *A Wordful Child*
Margaret Mahy   *My Mysterious World*
Rafe Martin   *A Storyteller's Story*
Patricia McKissack   *Can You Imagine*
Laura Numeroff   *If You Give an Author a Pencil*
Jerry Pallotta   *Read a Zillion Books*
Patricia Polacco   *Firetalking*
Laurence Pringle   *Nature! Wild and Wonderful*
Cynthia Rylant   *Best Wishes*
Seymour Simon   *From Paper Airplanes to Outer Space*
Mike Thaler   *Imagination*
Jean Van Leeuwen   *Growing Ideas*
Jane Yolen   *A Letter from Phoenix Farm*

For more information about the Meet the Author books
visit our website at www.RCOwen.com or call 1-800-336-5588